Four "Bitter Pills"

For Feeling Better Fast

Copyright © 2009 Stephan P. Michener, LCSW

ISBN 978-1-60145-720-2

All rights reserved. No part of this publication may be reproduced, stored in a retrieval system, or transmitted in any form or by any means, electronic, mechanical, recording or otherwise, without the prior written permission of the author.

Printed in the United States of America.

BookLocker.com, Inc.
2009

Four "Bitter Pills"

For Feeling Better Fast

Stephan P. Michener, LCSW

Dedication

To
My Mother- colorful, compassionate, and caring
and
My Father- patient, kind and rational

Contents

Preface ix
Introduction - The Purpose of This Book 1
A Quick Start Guide to Feeling Better 5
Chapter One: The First Bitter Pill - You Can't Change Others but You Can Change You 7
Chapter Two: The Second bitter pill - Your Thoughts Cause Your Feelings 13
Chapter Three: Becoming Aware of Your Thoughts 25
Chapter Four: Do You Know Your ABC's? 35
Chapter Five: How to Determine if a Thought is Rational or Irrational - Looking at Thoughts From a New Perspective 45
Chapter Six: The Third bitter pill - Sometimes Your Thoughts are Irrational 53
Chapter Seven: The Fourth Bitter Pill - Talk back to Your Irrational Thoughts 67
Chapter Eight: A Prediction and A Challenge 83
Appendix A 87
Appendix B 89
References 93
About the Author 95

Preface

After providing counseling services to individuals, couples and families for more than 23 years I have become aware of what is helpful and what is not as helpful to the clients who have given me the privilege of working with them. Like fashion styles, approaches to therapy come and go and new trends replace yesterday's fads. I was trained as a therapist when family therapy was all the rage, and for my first several years that was the lens I used as I approached my work.

There were times when I had to ask myself "how is this helping." The truth is that many times the family therapy approach wasn't helping. Eventually many therapists abandoned family therapy and started looking for the next new thing.

I decided to ignore the latest trends in therapy technique and instead went back to some of the time tested approaches that had been around for decades. I had known about Cognitive Behavior Therapy since I was a college student and was amused by its founder Albert Ellis and the songs he played on the banjo with plenty of four letter words about the ways we humans make ourselves miserable. Yes, he was a showman, and his approach may have turned some people away. But beyond his outrageous, blunt style, there was solid reasoning in the approach he developed.

Cognitive Behavioral Therapy is empirically based. This means that the claims of its effectiveness can be proven through research and experimentation. There is solid evidence that it works and is helpful to those who learn it. For those of us who aren't convinced by theory alone, but instead want to know why something works, Cognitive Behavior Therapy provides provable answers.

My appreciation for having evidence as to why an approach in psychology works or doesn't comes from my study with John Mavromatis, PhD at St. John Fisher College. As a professor and student of research methods and statistics, Dr. Mavromatis would frequently give his standard answer "I don't know" when we'd ask him a question about something. After a moment of silence he'd follow up with his own question "how could we find out" and the conversation would turn to a research design that we could do to prove some hypothesis. In Cognitive psychology class he would frequently ask "how do you know what you think you know." I thank John for teaching me the wisdom of saying "I don't know" and the process and science for finding out.

Theory is not enough. There needs to be evidence. Cognitive Behavior Therapy has plenty of evidence to support its effectiveness. It's not just a therapy technique. It's a philosophy and a system of thought for helping us make sense out of life and manage our emotions.

Introduction - The Purpose of This Book

I hope that by reading this book you are able to make some simple changes in your life that will help you feel better than you do now.

The Title of this book is **Four "Bitter Pills" For Feeling Better Fast**. It has nothing to do with taking pills or medication. The bitter pills I speak of are purely metaphorical in that they represent four principles for maximum mental health. My intent is to convey to you that by accepting these four principles you can make dramatic changes in the way you feel and the relationships you have with others.

Now, even though there are no pills necessarily involved here, if your depression or anxiety is severe enough that you want to seek medication from your doctor, go ahead. Taking medication does not mean that you can't use the ideas in this book. I have many clients that take medication and benefit from counseling. If you take medication I would just caution you against thinking when your emotions improve, that the gains are due *only* to the medication. Sometimes clients tend to give their medication more credit than they do themselves. Realize that you may have had some role in helping yourself to feel better.

I wrote this book to help my clients who I see in therapy get a little more out of their therapy experience. However, I also hope that it can stand on its own and be helpful to you whether or not you are in therapy.

Some people learn by hearing and engaging in learning activity. But sometimes reading the ideas can offer an added boost because you the reader can go back and reread it again. For some, the printed word is the way they learn best.

There are of course many self help books that you can read, and some of them even contain some of the ideas you will read here. These ideas are not new or mysterious, nor are they a bunch of psychological mumbo-jumbo. These ideas come from the field of cognitive behavior therapy (CBT), and have been around for a long time. My hope is that I can present these ideas to you in a way that is straight forward, practical and that comes across as almost "common sense."

The thing I don't like about the term Cognitive Behavior Therapy (CBT) is that it sounds like something someone does to you. I've found that many people are uncomfortable with therapy or counseling in general because they are afraid that the therapist might do something to them. Some people think that a therapist can read their minds, or give them unconscious suggestions. No therapist or counselor can do that. I wouldn't like seeing a counselor if I thought they could do that and I don't imagine that you would either. Therefore, I call my approach Cognitive Behavioral SELF Therapy. As the therapist I don't do anything to you. I merely teach you an approach and help you learn it and practice it. For clients who are in counseling with me, I hope this book can help reinforce what we discuss in counseling sessions.

One way that I intend this book to be different from many of the self help books that you might read, is that I intend it to be brief. One self help book that I have in my office that uses a similar Cognitive approach, has over 700 pages. Another has over 400 pages. Getting a little briefer, I have another book that is just slightly over 200 pages. When

Four "Bitter Pills" For Feeling Better Fast

I have referred my clients to books I have often found that they start out strong, but usually don't end up finishing the book! They might be missing some good stuff there, but I can't blame them. Self help books can be boring to read. So I'll keep this book brief.

Although the book is brief the steps to feeling better are intended to be done in order. Each step or *bitter pill* builds upon the one that came before it. I encourage you to do each step in order. I will also encourage you to suspend judgment on whether these "bitter pills" can be helpful to you. This approach does not apologize for itself and it is not "wishy-washy" about knowing how to be helpful. You won't find a bunch of "maybe" here. But if you can swallow these bitter pills, and accept the "truth" in them you will see quick and effective results.

Just one more thing. Don't think that just because this is brief, there isn't some serious substance to be gained here. Like the game of chess or Othello which can be learned in about ten minutes, it can take a lifetime to master. I can present these ideas to you briefly and quickly, but you are the one that needs to put into practice what you read. You will truly get out of this what you put into it. Let's get to it.

A Quick Start Guide to Feeling Better

We all want answers fast. When we attend a lecture or read a book we want the speaker/author to get to the point. I'm going to start right at the beginning by giving you the conclusion. I call this the Quick Start Guide to Feeling Better.

When we buy a new technological device it usually comes with a Quick Start Guide to get us started. After we get the device up and running we can go back to the manual and get the details about how to fine tune the device. I see no reason why this manual on Cognitive Behavioral SELF Therapy can't offer you a quick start guide. My only CAUTION to you is that this is about changing something that you do and changing habits may require some further explanation, encouragement and fine tuning. Also this is a book about a technique for changing your feelings and behavior, and the technique does require some explanation. So after reading the eight steps below you can start doing them, but please read the fine details in the rest of the manual.

1. Swallow the first bitter pill: Accept the fact that you can't change someone else but you can change you. Stop wasting your time.
2. Swallow the second bitter pill: Accept the fact that your thoughts cause your feelings. No thing and no one else makes you have the feelings you do.
3. Do your ABC's and pay very close attention to the B's or BELIEFS/THOUGHTS. Write them down so you can study them and learn about your thoughts.
4. See the connection between how you think and how you feel and behave.

5. Swallow the third bitter pill: Apply the 5 rational criteria to your thoughts and accept the fact that some of these thoughts you have are irrational.
6. Identify the specific types of irrational thinking you are doing. Use the list of Types of Irrational Thoughts to identify them.
7. Swallow the fourth bitter pill: Talk back to yourself and develop alternative thoughts using the 5 rational criteria about the situation that you formerly had irrational thoughts about
8. Recognize how your feeling and behavior differs (becomes more calm) as a result of thinking using the 5 rational criteria.

Chapter One: The First Bitter Pill - You Can't Change Others but You Can Change You

For over twenty years I have been asked to engage in many conspiracies. No, I am not some high ranking government official or secret agent operative. I'm a therapist. Several times each week when I have a new client come to one of their first few appointments they present me with the details of their life. This person or that person is upsetting them. Their job is making them miserable. The economy is making them anxious. They are depressed about their marriage. The kids are driving them crazy.

They have sought out a professional therapist to advise them on how to change their situation. They hope that I can tell them the magical things to say or the magical things to do to make the troubling person(s), or thing(s) less disturbing. They want me to enter into the **conspiracy** to change someone or something else. "What can I do to get my husband to stop drinking?" "How can I handle my boss when she makes unrealistic demands on me?" "What can I do to get my girlfriend to come back to me?" "Is there a way I can help my wife stop spending so much money?" "How do I help my daughter see that her boyfriend isn't right for her?" "How can I feel better about my situation?" The list is endless but it's usually about changing someone else.

Early on in counseling we have to be clear that a counselor can not help you change someone else. It doesn't matter how much you love that person or how angry you are at them. You can't change them. It's not that they *can't* change. It's just that you can't *make* them change.

If you are my client and I am your counselor- I can't even change you. That's right. We counselors have no ability to change our clients. But all of our clients have the ability to change themselves. Contrary to the belief of some people, counselors are not master manipulators. Counselors are just guides. I will discuss this later in this chapter.

Locus of Control
The concept of "Locus of Control" is helpful in increasing our awareness of what we can control and what we can't. Things that are within our locus of control are things that we can have control over, like how fast we drive our car. Things that are outside of our locus of control are things that we have no control over, like how fast someone else drives their car. As a homework assignment I sometimes ask my clients to draw a big circle on a sheet of paper. I then tell them to put everything that is in their control inside the circle, and everything that is not in their control outside the circle.

Sometimes they come to the next appointment with several things written inside the circle and only a few things outside the circle. But often they return with only a couple of things inside the circle and most everything else outside the circle. In many cases though when we examine some of the things people put inside the circle we find things that really don't belong there because the person doesn't have control over them.

The point is that there are only a very few things that we are in total control of and our emotions are one of the things we have that control over. That's what this book is about. We don't have control over the behavior, actions or feelings of other people. When we give up trying to cause change in others it allows us to more effectively work on improving our own emotional state.

A client who I had assigned the locus of control homework reminded me of the Serenity Prayer. When she returned the following week she presented me with the sheet of paper with the circle on it, and inside the circle she had written the serenity prayer.

Serenity Prayer
God grant me the serenity
to accept the things I cannot change;
courage to change the things I can;
and the wisdom to know the difference.

Living one day at a time;
Enjoying one moment at a time;
Accepting hardships as the pathway to peace;
Taking, as He did, this sinful world
as it is; not as I would have it;
Trusting that he will make all things right
if I surrender to His Will;
That I may be reasonable happy in this life
and supremely happy with Him
Forever in the next.
Amen

--Reinhold Neibuhr

In my opinion we could all improve our state of emotional well being if we would continue to strive to know the difference between the things we cannot change and instead focus on the things that we can change. While this is a simple concept it can have a profound impact on our mental health.

The Therapist of OZ

As a therapist I like to think of myself as the Wizard of OZ. When many people hear the words *Wizard of OZ* they might be inclined to think of "the great and powerful" being who can read minds and influence future events. As you may recall from the book (by L. Frank Baum) and the movie about Dorothy and her friends (the Scarecrow, the Tin Man and the Cowardly Lion) went to the Emerald city to have a visit with the Wizard of OZ. After getting themselves all cleaned up and looking their best they went into the Wizard's grand hall.

The Wizard was a very powerful and great man who made it clear to them that they were bothering him with their requests for a heart, brain, courage and Dorothy's desire to return to her home in Kansas. He was a very busy and important man. However, the Wizard said that he might help them if they completed a task. He instructed them to go off and get the Wicked Witch's broomstick. Of course this set Dorothy, Toto and their friends off on a treacherous adventure to obtain the Witch's broom. The mission seemed to put them in great peril and eventually Dorothy was captured and held a prisoner in the Witch's castle being guarded by flying monkeys. Oh my!

Later, when her friend the Scarecrow was put on fire by the Wicked Witch, Dorothy threw water on the Scarecrow to put out the fire. Dorothy accidently managed to get some water on the witch, which of course caused her to melt (a happy coincidence). Who knew? It turned out that there was no love lost between the flying Monkeys and their boss, the Witch, and they presented Dorothy with the broomstick to keep as a symbol of her victory. "Hail Dorothy."

Four "Bitter Pills" For Feeling Better Fast

Upon their return to the Emerald City Dorothy and her friends were eventually given an audience with the Wizard whom they laid the broomstick before. Being such a great and important man he was not very impressed and as he was in the process of sending them away, Dorothy's little dog Toto pulled back the curtain of the Wizard's control booth. (I am not making this up). The Wizard said "Pay no attention to that man behind the curtain". This is one of my favorite movie lines of all time. What a spectacle. Toto had revealed that the great and all powerful Wizard of OZ was just an ordinary man. He wasn't a bad man, just a bad Wizard as he himself admitted.

Let's not forget why Dorothy and her band of bizarre friends were there in the first place. The Scarecrow wanted a brain, the Tin Man wanted a heart, the Cowardly Lion wanted courage, and Dorothy just wanted to go back home. The Wizard had absolutely no ability to give them any of these things. Remember I said I like to think of myself as the Wizard of Oz. I have no power to give my clients these things either. The Scarecrow, Tin Man, Cowardly Lion and Dorothy already had the things and qualities they were seeking. During their adventure the Scarecrow showed his brains by concocting a plan to rescue Dorothy. The Tin Man was shown to possess great enthusiasm. And the Cowardly Lion demonstrated himself to be filled with courage. As for Dorothy- she had never really been that far away from home as the entire fantastic tale was all in her head while she dreamt.

What a wonderful story this is, but it is also a great metaphor for our own lives. We each have what we need within us. Each of us is complete having the brain, the heart and the courage. We also have the ability to call wherever we are home. The problem is that we sometimes think that we don't have the intelligence, the motivation or the bravery. The things we think are what this book is about and it is also the focus of my work with my clients in therapy.

Conclusion
The first step to helping yourself feel better is to swallow the bitter pill that you can't change other people. Once you stop wasting your energy and time on trying to get others to change you can focus on the changes that you can make. Your feeling of being effective will immediately improve, since you will stop doing the impossible. You simply can not change someone else.

Like me you are like the Wizard behind the curtain. There are severe limitations to your powers. However, if you look close enough at what you do have, you are likely to find that the resources you need to feel better are already within you. You can change the way that **YOU** feel and behave, by changing the way you think.

Chapter Two: The Second bitter pill - Your Thoughts Cause Your Feelings

Stated very simply, the second bitter pill is that *your thoughts cause your feelings.*
To provide you a little more detail about what this means:
If you have a normal functioning brain, the vast majority of your feelings and behaviors are totally and completely caused by you and you ONLY! No person, place or thing causes you to feel or behave the way you do. Your feelings and behaviors are a direct result of your thinking.

The second bitter pill is so central to Cognitive Behavioral SELF Therapy that if you don't swallow this "bitter pill" then you should put this book down now, and don't waste anymore of your time.

If you do accept this "bitter pill," then I have some good news and some bad news for you. First the BAD NEWS: You will have no one else to blame for how you are feeling and behaving. You also can't blame a group of people, a thing or an event for how you feel. You will have to be completely responsible for how you are feeling and acting.

Now the GOOD NEWS. Because you are completely responsible for how you feel and behave, you can change the way you feel and behave. You don't have to wait for anyone or anything to change the way you feel and behave. You are the Master of your own emotional and behavioral destiny. You are empowered if you accept this bitter pill. You are an emotional and behavioral slave to someone or something else if you don't.

This premise is what makes it or breaks it for people in Cognitive Behavioral SELF Therapy. Most of the time when one of my clients is stuck in their progress in therapy it is because they have relapsed on this notion and they are caught up in the belief that "Someone or something else makes me feel..." Once they re-swallow the second bitter pill that says that "he, she, it or they do not cause my emotions," they are able to do something to change how they feel again.

Think about the power you give to someone or something else because you believe that they make you feel the way you do. Giving someone or something else that much power over how you feel doesn't seem like a good idea.

In Cognitive Behavioral SELF Therapy you accept responsibility for how you feel. This is why I have added the word SELF to Cognitive Behavioral Therapy. Sometimes clients even mistakenly tell me that I as a therapist have made them feel so much better. As flattering as they are trying to be to me, they are also discrediting themselves. I can't make my clients feel better or worse. They do it themselves. I only teach and help my clients practice some new skills. I'm like the coach, but you are the athlete who either performs well enough to succeed, or you recognize you have to keep practicing. It is always possible to become even better.

The notion that other people, places, or things causes us to feel the way we do, is so predominate in our culture. Think of song titles like "You make me feel so young," "You make me feel like a Natural Woman," "You Light Up My Life," and "You are the Sunshine of My Life" to name just a few. Think of all the times you've said your self or heard someone else say "it makes me feel..."

The idea that our thoughts alone are what causes us to feel the way we do is not an easy concept to digest- that's why I call it a Bitter Pill. Changing the way you look at your everyday experiences and the emotions you have is not something that happens with the wave of a hand. On the other hand, it's not magical or mysterious either.

What are emotions and where do we experience them?
It might be helpful in your digestion of the second bitter pill if we briefly address the question of what emotions are and where we experience them. We have already established that your thoughts cause you to experience the emotions that you feel. But what are feelings and where do they originate from?

Whether we refer to them as feelings, emotions, affect, or mood it's all pretty much the same thing. We feel depressed or have anxious emotions, or an angry mood. Sometimes we might feel euphoric or happy and joyous. We describe our emotions as good or bad. What we really mean of course is that some of our emotions (depressed, angry, anxious, guilt) are undesirable and we'd like to feel them less, and other emotions (happy, love, contentment) are desirable and we'd like to feel them more.

Emotions aren't good or bad. They are just normal states that all people experience at one time or another. The problem comes when we experience *too* much of certain emotions. For instance too much depression, or anxiety, or anger, or guilt can be problematic and can prevent us from doing the things that we want to do in life.

In some psychotherapy schools of thought therapists are discouraged from asking their clients why they feel like they do. Those therapists follow the principle to just accept the client's feelings for what they are. They intentionally don't ask their clients why they feel the way that they do. Is *this* how we go about helping people feel better? To me this seems like the "bury your head in the sand approach" to helping people manage their emotions. Fortunately there are other ways to help people manage their feelings. The Cognitive/Behavioral school of thought is a useful and well proven method that has helped people for many years.

If we want to do something about the way we feel we have to ask where our feelings come from. A therapist asking someone why they feel the way they do is not the same thing as denying them the right to feel that way. It also isn't saying that it's wrong to feel that way. If you come to me and tell me you're depressed and I ask "where does the depressed feeling come from," I am not telling you that it's wrong to feel depressed. I'm just looking for what might be the source of your depression so that I can help you not feel as depressed. Doesn't it make sense to you that in order to help you change the emotional state that you're in we need to know how you got into that state in the first place?

Sometimes though my clients come to me and they are feeling sad or irritable or anxious and when I ask them what is causing these emotions- they aren't sure. To them it seems like it just comes on them from out of the blue. Fortunately Cognitive Behavioral Therapists have studied these things and are fairly certain that emotions do come from someplace. If you went to see your doctor about some symptoms you were experiencing you would want to know that your doctor either knew where the symptoms were coming from, or at least had a way of finding out what was causing them. In Cognitive Behavioral Therapy we have scientifically proven evidence about where emotions come from, which also helps us understand how to help people quickly and effectively change unwanted emotions.

Your Emotions and Feelings Come From Your Brain
It's funny that when we express emotions of love and fondness on Valentine's day we often use the symbol of a heart. We sometimes tell each other that we love one another "with all my heart." People are sometimes said to have died from a "broken heart." There's even a song that expresses it's emotion "straight from the heart." So it might seem that emotions originate in the heart. They don't. Your heart pumps blood, it's definitely not the source of your emotions. So what is the source of your emotions?

Have you ever seen one of those real-life medical TV shows where a neurosurgeon is doing brain surgery and the patient is awake on the operating table? With some mild electrical stimulation the surgeon can cause the patient to cry or laugh. These behaviors are representations of the emotional state that the patient experienced as a result of electrical stimulation to a specific part of the brain. This phenomenon demonstrates for us exactly where our emotions come from. Our emotional experiences happen in the brain.

Further evidence of the fact that our emotions come from our brains is that the antidepressants and other psychotropic medications that doctors prescribe act on specific chemicals called neurotransmitters- in the brain. Clearly, it is in your brain that you experience your emotions. Interestingly it is also in your brain that you think and *give meaning and interpretation to the events that you experience*. Is it any wonder then that there would be a connection between the thinking that goes on in your brain and the emotions that are created by your brain?

Four "Bitter Pills" For Feeling Better Fast

Very simply stated what happens to create our emotions is that we experience events in our daily lives which we *give meaning and interpretation to*. In other words we think about the events by assigning words to them. This activity usually goes on in the left hand side of our brains where our language center is (if we are right handed). Because the two sides of our brains are connected and they communicate with each other, the words that we have assigned in the left hand side of our brains to the events we have experienced get translated into non-verbal expressions on the right hand side of our brains. These non-verbal expressions are what we experience as emotions. As you will see, the words which we use to express our thoughts are of utmost importance in determining the emotions that we experience.

Just in case you were thinking that the only way to change the way you feel is through electrical stimulation of the brain or medication, there are definitely other ways. For some people medication and ECT might be the only way to help change the way they feel. However, the vast majority of people with problematic feelings of depression, anxiety, anger or guilt do not require those treatments. Fortunately, there are things that you can do to make some minor changes in your brain that do not require medication, ECT or surgery. Cognitive Behavioral Therapy is one such approach that aims at making changes in your brain which help you to regulate your emotions.

There have been numerous studies using brain scanning technology that have shown actual changes in brain electrical activity among patients who have received Cognitive Behavioral Therapy. One often cited research study conducted in 1977 by Aaron Beck, MD and colleagues found that the improvements made by patients receiving cognitive therapy was similar to the improvements made by patients receiving antidepressant drug therapy. More impressive was the fact that the people who received Cognitive therapy continued to show improvement after the therapy was over. The individuals just taking medications often lost the gains they experienced once discontinuing the medications.

In Cognitive Behavioral SELF Therapy we have a scientifically proven approach that has been clinically demonstrated to be effective. The effectiveness of Cognitive Therapy demonstrates that non medical interventions directed at thinking activity in the brain is as effective as many of the antidepressant medications being used today to help people manage their excessive and unwanted emotions.

A WORD about emotions
You will notice that in this book I am using some very specific words for the emotions that people experience. I limit the number of emotions I talk with my clients about to six words to describe the emotions. The six emotions are: Depression, Anxiety, Guilt, Anger, Happiness, and Calm.

You might be wondering why I don't include other feeling words like frustrated, disappointed, dissatisfied, content, agitated, irritable, annoyed, or the hundreds of other words you can think of to describe emotions people have. Why do I limit the words to the six mentioned? There are two reasons for this.
1) These six feeling words are the "boiled down" essence of all the other feeling words you could think of. They are the base emotion of other feeling words. Also one, two or more of these six words could be combined to describe

the other emotion words. For instance frustration might be considered to be a combination of anger and depression. Contentment might be a combination of calm and happiness. I believe it is helpful to talk in terms of the base emotion.
2) Limiting ourselves to these six words to describe our emotions helps us focus on what is more important than the emotions themselves, the thoughts that cause the emotions. By using more words to describe emotions we risk becoming distracted from increasing our awareness of our thoughts.

I recommend that you try to limit yourself to these six words when you describe how you feel. When you feel disappointed ask yourself which of the six "boiled down" words you might use as substitutes for "disappointed." Might you be feeling a combination of depressed, anxious, guilt and anger?

Do all of my feelings come from my thinking in my brain?
There are *some* people who have difficulty in regulating their emotions due to severe physiological conditions. There are people who have brain injuries and other organic causes behind their severe depression, anxiety, anger and guilt. For these people medical interventions including some fairly heavy duty medications are most likely the most appropriate interventions. (Note: Not all antidepressant medications including some of the Selective Serotonin Reuptake Inhibitors would be considered "heavy duty"). These organic/physiological conditions are not the focus of this book. Furthermore, most people who struggle with unwanted emotions do *not* have organic causes for their depression, anxiety, anger or guilt. For them, the approach described in

this book may be helpful. So even if you are taking an SSRI medication for your emotions this approach may have something to offer you.

Medications and the Placebo Effect
Most people do have normal healthy brains that are not controlled by drug or alcohol dependency or some sort of disease state. If your brain is being controlled by a disease state like psychosis, dementia, lesions or tumors, then Cognitive Behavioral Therapy is not for you. But you might say "I have a chemical imbalance that causes me to feel the way I do." If that's absolutely true see a medical doctor. But in all honesty how can you be sure you have a chemical imbalance. The only way that I know of to be absolutely certain is to do a brain biopsy which may have some serious side effects (like death).

Many people come to the conclusion that because they feel better after taking a psychotropic medication like an antidepressant or anti-anxiety agent that they must have had a chemical imbalance. From a hard science point of view this conclusion may not be true. While the depression or anxiety may be reduced, a researcher would still ask the questions about what caused the reductions of symptoms. Was it the actual medication that caused the change or was it some other variable? One frequent variable at play here is the "placebo effect."

I have seen many clients in my practice over the years that came to their therapy appointment after taking their newly prescribed Selective Serotonin Reuptake Inhibitor (SSRI) for a few days, who have told me they feel much better as a result. That is an interesting proclamation since we know that most SSRI's require taking them for three to four weeks before there is therapeutic benefit. Most likely in these cases the client is THINKING that because they are taking a medication that is supposed to decrease their depression or anxiety, they actually *feel* less depressed or anxious. It is quite possible that what is at work here is the placebo effect. The bottom line is that unless we do a brain biopsy we can't know for sure, and ethics and common sense won't allow absolute certainty.

Where do behaviors come from?
Now that we have established that our thinking causes us to have an emotional response or feeling, what if we want to change our behavior? Is it possible for us to behave without thinking or feeling?

In Cognitive Behavioral SELF Therapy our view is that all behavior happens *after* some thought and some emotional response. Both emotions and behavior are believed to be CONSEQUENCES of our thoughts. Usually our emotions have formed and it is the emotion that creates the motivation to take action. As an example of this consider the fight or flight response. When an individual experiences a threatening situation they immediately begin to interpret and evaluate the potential danger of the circumstances. This is their thinking. Based on what the individual's thoughts are about the perceived threat, they begin to experience emotions. Often times when a person has evaluated a situation as dangerous they begin to feel anxiety and sometimes anger. These feelings of anxiety and/or anger then result in behavior which may be either fight or flight.

Cognitive Behavior Therapy teaches that behavior is the consequence of feeling, and that feeling is the consequence of thought. If we were to map it out it would look like this:

EVENT → THOUGHT → EMOTION → BEHAVIOR

Conclusion
In this chapter I have made the case for the bitter pill that **your thoughts cause your feelings.** *If you have a normal functioning brain, the vast majority of your feelings and behaviors are totally and completely caused by you and you ONLY! No person, place or thing causes you to feel or behave the way you do. Your feelings and behaviors are a direct result of your thinking.*
This is the second bitter pill for you to digest on your journey to feeling better. Without accepting this second bitter pill, the third and the fourth bitter pills won't be helpful to you because what follows builds upon this premise. If you are still struggling with the idea that your thoughts cause you to feel the way you do, please go back and make sure you understand the points made in this chapter. I encourage the clients that I see in therapy to challenge the ideas presented here. On several occasions when I have asked them to "tell me where these ideas are wrong," they have started out to argue against them, but eventually come to realize that there is truth in this concept. One client once stated "How could it not be true?"

If you do accept the second bitter pill, it's time to work at increasing your awareness of your thoughts and how they determine how you feel.

Chapter Three: Becoming Aware of Your Thoughts

So if you have digested that your feelings are the result of your thoughts then it's time to get down to the business of recognizing your thoughts. That might sound strange to you that I would suggest that you have to become aware of your thoughts. You might ask me "Aren't people always aware of what they are thinking?" Well the answer is that people usually always have some form of mental activity going on which we would call thinking. However, just having thoughts happening does not necessarily mean that the person thinking them is separating them from the rest of their experiences which include their emotions and behaviors. The challenge here is to recognize your thoughts as being separate from your emotions and behavior. In this chapter I hope to show you a way to become more aware of your thoughts and separate them from your emotions.

Before we can even have mental activity going on in our brains we need to have something to think about. Something has to trigger us. We refer to this as a stimulus or stimulation. But for our purposes we will simply call this an EVENT. Something happens and our brains can then begin to think about it. However, not only does some event happen, but we have to be AWARE of it, in order for our brains to think about it.

Once we are AWARE of an event, then our mental activity begins. We start to think about the event that we are aware of. We have our interpretations, impressions, thoughts, perceptions and BELIEFS about the event. This is our thinking.

As a result of the thoughts and beliefs that we have, we then experience emotions which sometimes lead us to various behaviors. These emotions and behaviors are referred to as CONSEQUENCES. They are consequences of our thinking and beliefs.

Cognitive Therapies teach us to be aware of what are called the ABC's of our emotions/behaviors.

A stands for our AWARENESS OF AN EVENT

B stands for our BELIEF OR THOUGHT ABOUT THE EVENT

C stands for our EMOTIONAL AND/OR BEHAVIORAL CONSEQUENCES

These ABC's happen in sequential order. Generally most people are pretty good at recognizing the events they are aware of and they are pretty good at acknowledging their feelings and behaviors. What we aren't skilled at recognizing is our BELIEFS and THOUGHTS which lead to our emotions.

In fact it is very common for people to confuse their thoughts and their emotions. People often will state "I feel…" and then will go on to tell what they think. Consider this example: Have you ever asked someone how they felt about something or have you told someone about how you felt about something. It might go something like this:

John: "So Bill, how do you feel your team will do this season?"

Bill: "Probably not so well. Our pitching still isn't what it needs to be and there's no way we can make it in our division without a better bull pen. I'm not holding my breath and I'm not holding much hope."

This is a classic example of Bill not telling John how he feels but rather what he THINKS. He is giving his reasoning as to why he feels hopeless.

Here's another example of confusing thoughts with feelings:

Kevin : "What seems to be bothering you Mary?"
Mary : "I just feel that you don't listen to what I have to say and when I give you my opinion you do the exact opposite of what I want."

Mary has not told Kevin what she feels. She's told him what she THINKS but she labeled it as a feeling. We might guess that Mary either feels angry or depressed or a combination of the two, but she hasn't said that specifically. She has only told Kevin what she is thinking that might cause her to feel the way she does.

Here's another example of confusing thoughts and feelings.

Ted: "Hey Pat, are you angry at me?"
Karen: "I feel you are a phony. You said you'd call me and once again you didn't do what you said you would."
Even though Ted asked if Karen was angry (feeling), and then Pat used the words "I feel," she told Ted what her thoughts were, but not her feeling.

Differences Between Thoughts and Feelings

The difference between thoughts and feelings is that thoughts usually require multiple words to express. Feelings on the other hand can usually be expressed in one word. Feelings include words like depressed, happy, anxious, guilty, angry and calm. Thoughts are our interpretations, perceptions and explanations of how we process events we have experienced. Because they are explanations they require multiple words to express. Thoughts cause the feelings we have so it is extremely important that we be aware of them. But my main point here is that thoughts and feelings are different and in order to help yourself feel better you have to see the difference.

So here is an exercise for you to do. This is the classic ABC homework that many cognitive therapists use with their clients. It may seem cumbersome at first, but the more you do it the faster you'll recognize the difference between your thoughts and your feelings. Also, I want you to know that after doing this on paper several times you will begin to be able to do it in your head and won't need to put it on paper. But for now do it on paper.

In the three columns below what you do is take an event you recently experienced that may have resulted in you getting upset, saddened or anxious. In the A column provide a few words about what happened. **Be certain to stick to the facts about what happened.** Ask yourself if a camera or a tape recorder would verify how you describe the event in column A. Include nothing else other than what could be observed or heard. Stick to the facts!

In the B column write down some of the many thoughts you might have had about the event. For every event you record I would hope that you could identify at least four or five distinct thoughts about what you were aware.

In the C column record how you felt and behaved. Remember that a feeling can generally be summed up in one word. Beware of the tendency to explain how you felt with multiple words. Many people have the tendency to record some of their thoughts in the Consequence column. Be sure to keep thoughts in the B column.

I have provided a brief example of how I might have done this one night when my hot water heater leaked all over my basement.

Awareness of the Event	Belief/Thought about the Event	Consequences (Emotions/Behaviors)
Brushing my teeth. Not much water coming out. Went to the basement, found water all over the floor.	1) I can't believe this. This stinks. It's always something. 2) Things never go right for me. I can't get a break. 3) This is going to cost a fortune to fix. 4) What a stupid idiot I am. I should've replaced that water heater last year. 5) I'll probably get ripped off	Angry Anxious Depressed Slammed the mop on the floor Yelled at my wife to "stay out of my way

	getting a new one installed. 6) This is the worst thing that could've happened.	

As you can see from my example I have recorded the event that happened, the thoughts I was having about the event, and the feelings and behaviors I might have engaged in during the event. My feelings were a combination of Angry, Anxious and depressed. It wasn't that I was necessarily clinically depressed, but depressed is a *word* that might describe my mood just the same.

Now you try to record your thoughts and feelings related to a couple of situations/events you have experienced. Some people find it easier to do this exercise by recording the event that they were aware of first, followed by what their emotional and behavioral consequences were. THEN they go back to the BELIEF/THOUGHT column and record what thoughts they might have had. It doesn't matter what order you do this in. It can be A-B-C, but it could also be A-C-B. Don't get hung up on it because the whole point of this exercise if for you to become more aware of what your thoughts might have been that cause you to feel the way you do.

Sometimes clients tell me they weren't really sure what their thoughts were. That is okay. My question to help them fill out the BELIEF column is "What do you think you *might* have been thinking?" It's okay to conjecture. Chances are if you can make some plausible guesses you will begin to recognize the thoughts you were actually having. In

Cognitive therapies we refer to this apparent lack of awareness of what one was thinking as "*automatic thinking.*" Because thoughts can happen so rapidly and within nanoseconds it can seem like they weren't even there. Just remember this exercise is about becoming more aware of your thoughts.

You can use the space below for this exercise, and there is also a form in the appendix for you to use.

Awareness of the Event	**Belief/Thought about the Event**	**Consequences (Emotions/Behaviors)**

The above exercise is of utmost importance. I use the analogy that it is the frame of the Cognitive Behavioral SELF Therapy house. If you do not do this exercise accurately you may likely not get the benefit of this approach to managing your emotions and behaviors. If you're not sure about how you are doing the exercise speak with a cognitive therapist about it. You want to be sure you are seeing the difference between your thoughts and your feelings. Eventually you will be able to do this in your head, but it may take quite a bit of practice for you get there. Keep at it and make sure you've mastered this exercise before moving on.

Isn't this just Semantics?
The words we use to describe our thoughts and feelings are of ULTIMATE IMPORTANCE. Language is produced from the left side of your brain (if you are right handed). As we have discussed before your emotional experience also comes from your brain (not your heart). And your brain also directs your body to engage in physical actions (behaviors). When we express our emotional experiences we use language and behaviors. This is why we need to pay very close attention to the words we use to describe our emotional reactions. In fact it is through paying more attention to the words we use that we are better able to manage our emotions.

Dr. Maxie Maultsby, Jr. in his book *Rational Behavior Therapy*, points out that some clients protest that cognitive therapy is "just semantics," as if the words we use don't really matter. Dr. Maultsby responds "Where healthy emotional and other self-control is concerned, it's never *just* semantics; it's always *all* semantics." The words we use to express our thinking, either out loud or in our silent thoughts, not only reinforces how we feel, but **CREATES** how we feel.

By translating our thoughts into words and expressing them either to others or just silently to ourselves we take a big step towards managing our emotions and behaviors. This is why at the beginning of Cognitive Behavioral SELF Therapy we write out our emotional ABC's as you have learned to do so above. Please be aware that this is just the first step. However, once you take this step you are getting closer to what you need to do to manage your emotions and behaviors.

Conclusion
Awareness of the thoughts that we have is not always so obvious for most people. You have to put some effort into developing more awareness of the things you are thinking. This may sound strange to you at first, but consider this example. Do you have to think about what side of the road you drive your can on? Probably not. You have been doing it for so long that it is automatic. But you still are thinking as you drive your car down the road. It's just that the mental activity and thoughts of your brain happen without much effort on your part. However, if you were to go to England and drive over there, all of a sudden you would become much more aware of the thoughts you would be having. This would be because you would be in a new situation, and driving on the other side of the road.

In order for you to become more aware of the thoughts that run through your brain, and to become aware that your thoughts are separate from your feelings, this chapter has presented you with the ABC exercise. It is the foundation of everything that follows in this book. The next chapter will give you more specific examples to help you begin to do your own ABC exercises.

Chapter Four: Do You Know Your ABC's?

The ABC's are the building blocks of Cognitive Behavioral SELF Therapy and therefore it is crucial you understand them and be able to do them in a way that will be helpful to you. Without knowing your alphabet you couldn't be reading these words. Without being able to do the ABC exercise correctly you can't benefit from the approach to feeling better presented in this book.

This chapter will give you several examples of both right and wrong ways of doing the ABC exercise. I will show you a wrong example, followed by some comments, and then give you a corrected example. Keep in mind it is not my intention to evaluate the thoughts presented here, but rather to just demonstrate the wrong vs. correct way of doing the exercise.

Example 1
WRONG

Awareness of the Event	Belief/Thought about the Event	Consequences (Emotions/Behaviors)
Found husband looking at porn on the computer. He shouldn't be doing that. What a jerk.	1) This proves he doesn't love me. 2) He's a scum bag. 3) I can't believe this happened.	Angry Depressed Yelled and stormed out of the room

A common mistake that people make in doing their ABC's is found in the example above. In the A section the woman has included some of her thoughts about her husband. These need to be moved to the B section.

CORRECT

Awareness of the Event	Belief/Thought about the Event	Consequences (Emotions/Behaviors)
Found husband looking at porn on computer.	1) This proves he doesn't love me. 2) He's a scum bag. 3) I can't believe this happened. 4) He shouldn't be doing that. 5) What a jerk.	Angry Depressed Yelled and stormed out of the room

Example 2
WRONG

Awareness of the Event	Belief/Thought about the Event	Consequences (Emotions/Behaviors)
Police officer pulled me over and gave me a ticket.	1) I was just going 5mph over the speed limit 2) I feel he should go after serious criminals 3) I asked him to let me go.	Anxious Guilty Asked him to let me go this time This is what I pay taxes for?

In example 2 the A section is fine. However, the second thought is labeled as a feeling and it really is a thought which could be expressed as "He should go after more serious criminals." In the C column is another thought (This is what I pay taxes for?) that should be in the B column. Also, the third thought "I asked him to let me go" is really a behavior.

CORRECT

Awareness of the Event	Belief/Thought about the Event	Consequences (Emotions/Behaviors)
Police officer pulled me over and gave me a ticket.	1) I was just going 5mph over the speed limit 2) He should go after serious criminals 3) Is this what I pay taxes for?	Anxious Guilty Asked him to let me go this time

Example 3
WRONG

Awareness of the Event	Belief/Thought about the Event	Consequences (Emotions/Behaviors)
Janice asked me to work some extra overtime. She is trying to get me to quit by pissing me off.	1) I'm working too many hours 2) I never get any time off anymore 3) I told her to "go to hell" 4) I can't stand this 5) I felt like kicking the door	Depressed What am I supposed to do? I miss my family Angry

In example 3 the person includes information in the A column that couldn't be verified with a "camera check" of what really happened. There is no proof that "She is trying to get me to quit by pissing me off." This might be a thought, and needs to be moved. In the Belief column the statement "I told her to go to hell" needs to be put in the Consequence column since it was a behavior. Also the statement that "I felt like kicking the door" is actually a thought the person had, not a feeling. In the Consequence column the statements "what am I supposed to do?" and "I miss my family" are actually thoughts and need to be moved to the Belief column. Notice how there are actually a lot more thoughts in the correct example than were originally recorded in the wrong example.

CORRECT

Awareness of the Event	Belief/Thought about the Event	Consequences (Emotions/Behaviors)
Janice asked me to work some extra overtime.	1) I'm working too many hours 2) I never get any time off anymore 3) I miss my family 4) I can't stand this 5) I thought about kicking the door 6) What am I supposed to do? 7) She is trying to get me to quit 8) She is trying to piss me off	Depressed Angry I told her to "go to hell"

Beware of the rhetorical question

Dictionary.com defines a rhetorical question as "a question asked solely to produce an effect or to make an assertion and not to elicit a reply." Rhetorical questions don't usually have a response, but if they do, the response is usually fairly obvious. What's key in the above definition is that a rhetorical question is intended to "make an assertion." When someone asks a rhetorical question they are making a statement and expressing a thought.

In example 2 above the person asks the rhetorical question "Is this what I pay taxes for?" Well the answer is an obvious yes, it is what *some* of your taxes go for. But most likely the person is expressing the thought that they don't like paying taxes for police officers to stop them and give them speeding tickets.

In example 3 the person expresses the thought "What am I supposed to do?" Again this is a rhetorical question. Perhaps the statement that is being made here is "I don't know what I am supposed to do." Maybe the thought is "I feel torn between my job and my family." In either case the rhetorical question was concealing a thought that the person had.

As you do your own ABC's watch out for rhetorical questions. When you find yourself asking one, substitute it with the statement or assertion that you are trying to make. Ask yourself what is the thought behind the question.

Example 4
WRONG

Awareness of the Event	Belief/Thought about the Event	Consequences (Emotions/Behaviors)
My daughter asked me to take her to the store because she needed something for school.	1) She's always asking me to spend money 2) What does she think? I'm made of money 3) This is terrible 4) Am I supposed to let her go without what she needs?	Angry Anxious Guilty Told her we'd go when she cleans her room

Four "Bitter Pills" For Feeling Better Fast

In example 4 the Awareness of the event column is fine because the facts are stated with nothing else. In the Consequences column the person has indicated how they felt and what they did. The problem here is in the Belief column where there are a couple or rhetorical questions "What does she think? I'm made of money." And "Am I supposed to let her go without what she needs?"

CORRECT

Awareness of the Event	Belief/Thought about the Event	Consequences (Emotions/Behaviors)
My daughter asked me to take her to the store because she needed something for school.	1) She's always asking me to spend money 2) She thinks I'm made of money 3) This is terrible 4) I can't let her go without what she needs for school	Angry Anxious Guilty Told her we'd go when she cleans her room

Example 5
WRONG

Awareness of the Event	Belief/Thought about the Event	Consequences (Emotions/Behaviors)
My girlfriend called right before I was to pick her up and cancelled our	1) She's always doing stuff like this 2) She doesn't want to see me	Angry Anxious Depressed Went out with my buddy and got drunk. I

date. She knows I hate this last minute crap. She does this to piss me off.	anymore 3) She should give me more notice 4) I can't stand this crap 5) What does she expect me to do? 6) I feel this is too much drama 7) I'll show her I don't need her 8) This is a terrible situation	showed her

It's great that the person in the above example was able to identify so many thoughts that they might have had. There's even a couple of thoughts in the A column and a thought in the C column. Notice that there's also a rhetorical question in the B column that needs to be rewritten as a statement. Also there is the acknowledgement of a feeling of guilt in the B column. A much more accurate representation of this person's ABC's follows.

CORRECT

Awareness of the Event	Belief/Thought about the Event	Consequences (Emotions/Behaviors)
My girlfriend called right before I was to	1) She's always doing stuff like this	Angry Anxious Depressed

Four "Bitter Pills" For Feeling Better Fast

pick her up and cancelled our date. It was right as I was on my way out the door	2) She doesn't want to see me anymore 3) She should give me more notice 4) I can't stand this crap 5) She wants me to get angry. She does this to piss me off. 6) She knows I hate this last minute crap 7) I think this is too much drama 8) I'll show her I don't need her 9) This is a terrible situation	Went out with my buddy and got drunk. Guilt

Notice that the A column contains "just the facts." The Belief/Thought column has just what this person was thinking, and the rhetorical question has been replaced by the person's thought statement that he believes his girlfriend does this to get him angry. Also his previous statement that he "feels" this is too much drama has been replaced with his acknowledgement that he "thinks" this is too much drama. Finally, his statement in the Consequences column that "I showed her" has been moved to the Belief/Thought column where it becomes "I'll show her I don't need her."

Conclusion
Please keep in mind that in the above examples I have not made any comments about the actual thoughts themselves. We will discuss evaluating thoughts in the next chapter. My main concern at this point is that you know how to do the ABC's correctly and that you recognize the difference between what really happened, what you thought about it, and how you felt and behaved.

Since everything that follows in this book is based on doing the ABC's correctly, and demonstrating that you are aware of the differences between thoughts and feelings, it is crucial that you can do these accurately. If you are confident that you have a clear understanding of this then it is time to take the next step.

Chapter Five: How to Determine if a Thought is Rational or Irrational - Looking at Thoughts From a New Perspective

In order for Cognitive Behavioral SELF Therapy to work for you, you have to be doing your ABC's that were explained in Chapter 3. I don't mean doing them in your head. You have to do them on paper so you can LOOK at them. Eventually you will be doing your ABC's in your head, but for now keep doing them on paper. Like any new learned skill you have to do it methodically at first before it will seem natural to you. *I can not emphasize enough the importance of doing your ABC's on paper.*

Also by putting your thoughts about the events you experience down on paper you will see how your thoughts are causing your emotions and behaviors. This is key because now I am going to teach you how to evaluate your thoughts. That's right: I said EVALUATE your thoughts. I'm not going to evaluate them, and I don't want you to go ask someone else to evaluate them. YOU are going to EVALUATE your own thoughts.

There are two ways you can evaluate your thoughts. Either your thinking is RATIONAL or IRRATIONAL. Your thoughts either make sense or they don't. The problem with evaluating our own thoughts is that we are biased. If you were to ask someone that you were having a disagreement with if their thoughts were rational or irrational, what do you think they'd say? What would you say about your own thoughts? We all tend to think our thoughts are perfectly rational. Thinking that all of your thoughts are perfectly rational is an irrational thought in itself. Even I as a therapist and practitioner of Cognitive Behavioral SELF Therapy have irrational thoughts sometimes.

What we need is an objective method to evaluate our thoughts that is consistent and can be applied over and over again. This is how we go about looking at our thoughts from a new perspective. By having a list of objective criteria that we can apply to our thoughts we can be fairly certain that we are evaluating our thoughts without bias. After applying this list of criteria you can determine if each and every thought you have is RATIONAL or IRRATIONAL.

Here are the criteria for a RATIONAL THOUGHT.
A RATIONAL THOUGHT;
    1.   is supported by objective fact
    2.   helps you maintain your physical health and well being
    3.   helps you reduce conflict with people you care about
    4.   helps you accomplish a task or goal that is important to you
    5.   helps you feel calm, accepting, at peace

CONVERSLY AN IRRATIONAL THOUGHT;
    1.   is not supported by objective fact
    2.   jeopardizes your physical health and well being
    3.   increases conflict with the people you care about
    4.   prevents you from accomplishing tasks and goals that are important to you
    5.   helps you feel more depressed, anxious, angry or guilty than you want to

Four "Bitter Pills" For Feeling Better Fast

In evaluating your thoughts you need to ask yourself if your thought is RATIONAL using the five criteria. If just one of the criteria is not present your thought is irrational and will cause you some emotional distress. To see this at work let's go back to the example I gave you when my hot water tank broke down and flooded my basement. As you will recall my thoughts and feelings were as follows (note that I left out the Awareness of the Event column);

Belief/Thought about the Event	Consequences (Emotions/Behaviors)
1) I can't believe this. This stinks. It's always something. 2) Things never go right for me. I can't get a break 3) This is going to cost a fortune to fix 4) What a stupid idiot I am. I should've replaced that water heater last year. 5) I'll probably get ripped off getting a new one installed 6) This is the worst thing that could've happened	Angry Anxious Depressed Yelled at my wife to "stay out of my way" Slammed the mop on the floor

Let's start with the first thought I had: "I can't believe this. This stinks. It's always something." You'll notice that this is actually three separate thoughts so let's break it down and look at the first thought: "I can't believe this."

Thought: "I can't believe this."
Rational Criteria
1) A rational thought is supported by objective fact. Of course I *can* believe it. I was standing in my basement with my feet wet. Telling myself that I can't believe it is just plain untrue. Therefore, there is not objective fact here and this thought doesn't meet one of the five criteria for a rational thought.
2) A rational thought Helps you maintain your physical health and well being. In this case my thought really doesn't immediately jeopardize my health and well being.
3) A rational thought Helps you reduce conflict with people you care about. This thought doesn't seem to have anything to do with my conflict with people I care about, but notice that eventually I did yell at my wife.
4) A rational thought Helps you accomplish a task or goal. Thinking and saying "I can't believe this" does nothing to help me get to the task at hand of cleaning up the mess and then getting to bed. Again the thought doesn't meet another criteria for a rational thought.
5) A rational thought Helps you feel calm, accepting and at peace. Thinking and saying "I can't believe this" doesn't do anything to calm me down, and accept the situation. Once again the thought doesn't meet one of the criteria for a rational thought.

You'll notice that my thought "I can't believe this" does not meet three of the five criteria for a rational thought. It does not meet criteria 1, 4 and 5. When we have a thought that does not meet all five criteria it is an irrational thought. In fact if the thought fails to meet **just one** of the five criteria, it is irrational.

Irrational thoughts are not supported by objective fact, do not help us to maintain our physical well being, don't help us reduce conflict with people we care about, don't help us accomplish a task or goal, and don't help us feel the way we want to.

Thought: "This stinks."
Rational Criteria
1) A rational thought is supported by objective fact. Actually there was no smell associated with the broken water heater, so this thought wasn't supported by objective fact and is already an irrational thought.

2) A rational thought Helps you maintain your physical health and well being. In this case my thought really doesn't immediately jeopardize my health and well being.

3) A rational thought Helps you reduce conflict with people you care about. This criteria doesn't necessarily apply here.

4) A rational thought Helps you accomplish a task or goal. Thinking that a broken water heater stinks doesn't do anything to accomplish the task at hand. Again this thought is irrational based on this criteria.

5) A rational thought Helps you feel calm, accepting and at peace. Again, thinking that "this stinks" doesn't help one feel the way they'd want to, and is another irrational thought.

Once again the thought that "This stinks" is proven to be irrational according to criteria 1, 4 and 5. It simply doesn't meet the criteria necessary for us to consider it a rational thought.

The key thing to recognize here is that by thinking irrational thoughts, we end up feeling either depressed, anxious, angry, guilty, frustrated, or some other unpleasant way. Do we want to feel unpleasant feelings? Obviously not. But still the thoughts that we have cause us to have these unpleasant emotions. So the thing to do is to work towards changing our thinking about the situation. We will discuss that later on. For now let's look at another thought I had when my water heater broke.

Thought: "Things never go right for me"
Rational Criteria
1) A rational thought is supported by objective fact. Do you think it is true that nothing has ever gone right for me? By thinking this I am telling myself something that is just not true. It doesn't help and it's an irrational thought because it's not true..
2) A rational thought Helps you maintain your physical health and well being. In this case my thought really doesn't immediately jeopardize my health and well being.
3) A rational thought Helps you reduce conflict with people you care about. This criteria doesn't necessarily apply here.
4) A rational thought Helps you accomplish a task or goal. Once again thinking this way doesn't help me accomplish the task of cleaning up and getting back to bed. Therefore, the thought is not rational.
5) A rational thought Helps you feel calm, accepting and at peace. If I believe that "things never go right for me" I

wouldn't feel calm, accepting or at peace. Again, another unmet criteria for a rational thought.

Hopefully by now you are getting the idea of how we use the five criteria to evaluate if our thoughts are rational or irrational. In the example I have provided here not one of the six thoughts I listed can be determined to be rational. They are all irrational thoughts. Most people have a combination of rational and irrational thinking. But the key is to recognize where the irrational thoughts are, so that they can be modified and not be upsetting to us.

What really happened
The truth is that when the hot water heater broke in my house I did think that "I should've replaced it last year." I also thought that it might be expensive to repair, and I was thinking that when I get up tomorrow to go to work, I won't have a place to shower. I definitely had a problem that I needed to solve. Fortunately as I was having some of these irrational thoughts that could've been quite upsetting, I began to use Cognitive Behavioral SELF Therapy on myself. I was aware of my irrational thoughts and that I needed to do something about them. I knew they would need to be replaced with rational thoughts that would keep me calm and goal oriented. By using the steps that I will describe in the next couple of chapters I was able to quickly replace my irrational thinking with rational thinking. As a result, in this situation I did not get upset and did not yell at my wife. I shut off the water, cleaned up the mess, discussed with my wife how we could solve the problem by calling a plumber in the morning, developed a plan to call a friend in the morning to ask if I could take a shower at their home before going to

work, and then went to bed and got a good night's rest. The Cognitive Behavioral SELF Therapy approach worked flawlessly and quickly.

Now I realize that a broken water heater is a relatively minor problem. Many people are facing events in their lives that are more serious and troubling to them than a flooded basement. But the method can be as helpful in those situations as it was here, and it can be used the same way. The key is to accept that our thoughts cause our feelings, and that some of our thoughts are irrational. We will discuss the necessity of swallowing the third bitter pill in the next chapter.

Conclusion
In this chapter we discussed that all thoughts are either rational or irrational. But just saying that a thought is rational or irrational isn't enough. That's why this chapter gave you 5 specific criteria for declaring a thought to be either rational or irrational. By using these same 5 criteria over and over for every thought we have, we can be more certain that we are not being subjective in our determination. What's also important is to acknowledge that a rational or irrational thought is not good or bad. All of us have both rational and irrational thoughts. The key is to know the difference.

Chapter Six: The Third bitter pill - Sometimes Your Thoughts are Irrational

Okay, so now you understand that Cognitive Behavioral SELF Therapy can help you recognize the differences between rational and irrational thoughts. That's all there is to feeling better and changing your mood. Right? Well not exactly.

It's one thing to be able to tell the difference between a rational and an irrational thought, BUT it's a whole other matter to begin replacing irrational misery producing thoughts with rational calming thoughts. Hopefully by now you've not only swallowed but have also digested the second bitter pill that your thoughts cause you to feel the way you do. You firmly accept that no other thing, person, group of people or place causes you to feel the way you do.

Now it's time to swallow the third bitter pill which is that *some of your thoughts are irrational*. Notice- I said some of your thoughts. They are not irrational because I say so, or because someone else told you that your thoughts are irrational. Some of your thoughts are irrational because they are not in keeping with the five rational criteria you read about in the last chapter. You now realize that if the thought doesn't meet even just one of the criteria for being rational, it's an irrational thought.

It's important enough to restate the criteria for an irrational thought.
An Irrational thought;
1. is not supported by objective fact
2. jeopardizes your physical health and well being

3. increases conflict with the people you care about

4. prevents you from accomplishing tasks and goals that are important to you

5. helps you feel more depressed, anxious, angry or guilty than you want to

If just one of these criteria holds true for the thought, it is IRRATIONAL. Being able to tell yourself that some of your thoughts are irrational is the third bitter pill for you to swallow. It's not that all of your thoughts are irrational all the time, just some of them some of the time. If you don't want to feel depressed, angry, anxious or guilty you have to identify your irrational thoughts because those thoughts cause your negative unwanted emotions.

What types of irrational thoughts do you have?
Knowing some of your thoughts are irrational is not enough. You also have to identify what type of irrational thoughts you are engaged in. There are many types of irrational thoughts and we all have certain types of irrational thoughts that we engage in over and over. When you recognize that one of your thoughts is irrational it's time to identify what form of irrational thinking you are engaged in. By identifying what type of irrational thought you have, you take one more step in sincerely convincing yourself that some of your thoughts are irrational.

Sometimes my clients ask "What does it matter what kind of irrational thought it is, as long as I recognize that my thought is irrational?" I believe that by giving your irrational thought a name it makes it more real to you, and might help prevent you from just dismissing it as a "harmless little irrational thought." By identifying it, it makes it matter more.

Four "Bitter Pills" For Feeling Better Fast

There is no such thing as a "harmless little irrational thought." Where one irrational thought exists there are likely to be more. One irrational thought can often times lead to another. Therefore I encourage you to give your irrational thinking a name and identify it for what type of irrational thought it is.

The other way that identifying the irrational thought is helpful is that it can help prove to you that you are not alone in thinking these irrational thoughts. Other people do the same kinds of irrational thinking as you do, and psychological researchers have clearly identified several distinct types of irrational thought. Those of us who study rational thought and who work as therapists helping others with irrational thoughts are not immune to having our own irrational thinking.

Perhaps the most important reason for identifying what types of irrational thoughts you have is that it is the first step towards developing increased rational thinking. If you know specifically what types of irrational thoughts you have you are aware of what changes you will need to make to your thinking. As you will see below the thought types are descriptive of what makes that type of thought irrational.

What follows is a list of 10 different types of irrational thoughts that I have compiled from various sources. Following the list is a brief explanation of each type of irrational thought.This list contains the most common types of irrational thoughts and the ones that are easiest to recognize. There are actually a few other types of irrational thoughts that can be found in the Appendix. Take a look at it and see if any of these types of irrational thoughts seem familiar to you.

Four "Bitter Pills" For Feeling Better Fast

1) All or None Thinking-
2) Overgeneralization-
3) Jumping to Conclusions-
    Mind Reading-
    Fortune Telling-
4) Irrational Labeling-
    Metaphorical comparisons-
5) Irrational Should Statements-
6) Confusing Needs with Wants-
7) Confusing Choosing To (Choice) with Having To (Force)-
8) Confusing Inability with Unwillingness-
9) Can't Stand-it-itis-
10) Catastrophizing-

Descriptions if Irrational Thought Types
Below is a brief description of each of the Irrational Thought types to help you become more aware of them.

All or None Thinking- This is thinking that is "black or white." When people think like this they describe events as being either all good or completely bad. There is no gray area. One might think, " this is the worst thing I have ever experienced." Another person might think "No one could possibly understand what I'm going through." Sometimes people falsely believe "everyone wants the same things in life" as if all people are the same.

Overgeneralization- These thoughts are often in the land of exaggeration. They come with words like "always" and "never." For instance someone might think "I always get the short end of the stick." Other times they might think "She always decides to do the opposite of what I want." Furthermore, they might think "I never get to decide what movie to see." The problem with overgeneralizations is that they usually are not true or supported by the facts.

Jumping to Conclusions- This is where people think that their predictions are accurate even when they don't have evidence to support their conclusions. Jumping to conclusions thinking often leads to feelings of anxiety. This "jumping to conclusions" is often in one of two forms.

Mind Reading- This is the belief that someone knows what someone else is thinking. It can be fairly mild and innocent like "I know you were disappointed when you didn't get that job." It can also be more problematic like when someone believes "You knew that would make me upset." Frequently mind reading involves attributing intentions to others, which are not known for sure. One person is assuming that they know what the other person is thinking.

Fortune Telling- These are thoughts where the person predicts what is going to happen in the future despite not having any solid proof for coming to that conclusion. A woman might think of her husband "I know he'll probably cheat on me at some point." Another person might create anxiety for themselves by thinking "it's just a matter of time before I get laid off."

Irrational Labeling- is when someone calls someone or something a name that it is not. People frequently refer to other people with irrational labels like a car driver who calls another motorist a "jackass." Since donkeys can't operate motor vehicles it is quite unlikely the other driver is a jackass. Often times the labels we give to other humans dehumanizes them, while irrationally the labels we give to inanimate objects sometimes give them human characteristics. I once referred to a golf ball that I hit poorly as a "bastard." The bottom line is that our labels for things are often inaccurate and contribute to our increasing the heat in our anger.

Metaphorical comparisons- are when we think that this situation is like something else. Often times it involves using an analogy. For instance a client once told me that her six year old daughter knew how to "push her buttons." Of course the metaphorical buttons don't exist and a more rational explanation might be that a six year old knows how to act like a six year old. Another client insisted that his supervisor "treated him like garbage" because he asked him to get some tasks done at work. Actually it seems like the supervisor might have treated him like a supervisee. The title of this book uses a metaphorical comparison to taking four bitter pills. When we think in metaphors or analogies there is the risk that our thinking may be inaccurate and can lead us to further upset.

Irrational Should statements-Sometimes there is confusion about why should statements are sometimes irrational. Clients will sometimes argue that their thought that something "should" happen is perfectly rational. For instance a parent might say that their child *should* listen to them and do as they are told. I agree completely if we are talking about doing something that they are expected to do in the future. The thought that "my child should be in by their curfew when they go out tomorrow night" is a rational statement. It is a rational use of *should* because it talks about an expectation for future behavior.

When should statements refer to past behavior that is when they are irrational. For instance the thought that "my child should've come in by their curfew last night" is an irrational statement. Why is it irrational? Keep in mind the first criteria for a rational thought is, that it has to be supported by objective fact. The thought that the child *should've* come in by the curfew is not supported by the objective fact that they didn't come in on time. No matter how much one insists that something *should've* happened the fact is that it didn't. When we think irrational should thoughts about other people it usually causes us to feel anger. When we think irrational should thoughts about ourselves it often leads us to feel guilty. So keep in mind that *should* thoughts about future events are probably rational, but *should* thoughts about past events are irrational.

Confusing Needs with Wants- There are only four things that any human absolutely needs for long term survival. These needs are food, water, shelter and sleep. Everything else in life is a "want." If I am hungry and really need to eat to survive I will eat anchovies out of the can even though I don't like anchovies. However, tonight I might *want* to have pizza for dinner. Listen to the things you say as well as what those around you say. You will notice that frequently people will state they *need* when what they really mean is they *want*." My children will often tell me "I need to go to the store to get something for school." It is irrational for them to think they need to go to the store when the more accurate and honest truth is that they want to go to the store to get the thing they need for school because they want to do well and be in good favor of the teacher.

Confusing Choosing To (Choice) with Having To (Force)- Another way that thinking can be irrational is when we confuse our choice to do something with thinking that we have to. There are very few things in life that you have to do. Most things that we do are completely by choice. Consider this question. If a robber came to you on the street and held a gun on you and told you to give him all your money, would you have to give him your money or would you choose to give him your money? You would probably choose to give him your money, but you wouldn't have to. But let's say that instead of asking you to give him your money, he grabbed your purse right out of your arms. Would you be choosing to give him your money or would you have to give him your money? Obviously in this situation there is no choice, you would have to under force. When you think about going to work it is likely that you tell yourself that you have to go to work. However, from a rational thought perspective you choose to go to work, because you want to keep your job so that you will continue to get paid and be able to afford the things you want.

Confusing Inability with Unwillingness- It is very common for people to think that they are *unable* to do something which they are actually *unwilling* to do. Let's say that you were invited to two parties that were occurring on the same day, at the same time. Would you be unable or unwilling to go to one and not the other? The rational answer is that you would be willing to go to one and unwilling to go to the other. It doesn't really matter why you would be willing to go to one and not the other. You might like the host better of the party that you are willing to go to. The simple fact is that you are unwilling to go to the other party. You can't even say that you *have* to go to the other party because you are *choosing* to go to that party and you are *unwilling* to go to the other party. If you were arrested and put in jail on your way to the party, then you could tell the person who invited you that you were *unable* to attend.

Can't Stand-it-itis- This is a term coined by Albert Ellis, PhD the founder of Cognitive therapy. Thinking that you *can't stand* an event is irrational because what do the words *can't stand* mean? Does it mean you will burst into spontaneous combustion or explode? Of course you won't. You might *prefer* to not be facing the event you are facing, but you will be able to stand it. A similar irrational thought is "I can't believe it." Does this mean you are unable to believe something or are you unwilling? Just like you can actually stand it, you can believe it too. Consider that when we think that I can't believe it we are saying that we are denying reality. That doesn't seem to be a rational thing to do. It also isn't a rational thought to tell yourself that you can't stand something that you can withstand, even if you would *prefer* to not have to deal with the event.

Catastrophizing- This is another one of Dr. Ellis's terms as is *awfulizing*. Thinking that an event is *awful, terrible,* or a *catastrophe* is irrational thinking. This type of irrational thought is also closely related to can't-stand-it-itis and overgeneralizations, because the thought is a gross exaggeration. Most importantly to understand about catastropphizing is that what makes an event terrible for one person is a subjective experience. It is not an *objective* reality. What one person experiences as an awful event may be experienced by someone else as a positive experience. Consider the example of a team that loses a championship game. In the locker room after the game they may hang their heads and talk about how terrible it was that they lost. Someone may be apt to think how awful it was to work as hard as they did all season only to end up losing the championship game. Meanwhile in the other locker room the celebration is underway as the members of that team pat each other on the back, and express their thoughts about how their hard work paid off. In this example what is awful, terrible or a catastrophe to one team, is a joy and a pleasure to the other team. A more rational thought about the loss is that it was unfortunate and disappointing. Ultimately though, our interpretation that an event is disappointing or unfortunate is our own subjective interpretation and not objective fact.

Do you recognize yourself having any of these types of irrational thoughts? As time goes on and you become more familiar with these types of irrational thoughts you can hopefully recognize when you are engaged in this type of thinking. Once you recognize that the thought is irrational, and you can identify what type of irrational thought it is, you are getting very close to making some changes in your thinking that will lead you to greater calmness and less conflict in you life. You will be more fully in control of your emotions.

Example of Irrational Thought Identification- Road Rage
So now let's take a common example that I'm sure many of you have either seen or engaged in yourself. "Road rage" is nothing more than feelings of anger that sometimes get acted out when we are driving our car. It can happen so quickly, but as I told you before, thoughts happen within milliseconds, and often times those thought patterns are so well rehearsed (automatic thinking) that we experience the emotion and engage in behaviors without stopping to question the rationality of the thinking that caused the emotion in the first place.

Four "Bitter Pills" For Feeling Better Fast

A	B	C
Awareness of Event	**Belief/Thought about the Event**	**Consequences (Emotions/Behaviors)**
Another car came very close to mine. I slammed on my breaks	1) That guy almost killed me (all or none thinking) 2) He's an S.O.B. (irrational labeling) 3) He should've been watching where he's going (Irrational Should) 4) Someone's always trying to get in my way (Overgeneralization) 5) I can't stand this. I won't tolerate this crap (Can't-Stand-It-it is) 6) Now I'll be late. This will ruin my whole day (Fortune telling) 7) This sucks. It's terrible (Catastrophising)	Anger Anxiety Shake my fist, yell, throw the finger.

Clearly there's a whole bunch of irrational thinking going on in this example.

Thought 1: The other driver did not almost kill me. His car did come close to mine and I might have hit him had I not slammed on the brakes. But the fact remains that he did not almost kill me.

Thought 2: I also doubt that he is a "son of a bitch" because a bitch is a female dog and as far as I know a human male cannot be birthed by a female canine. This flies in the face of objective reality and is clearly an irrational label.

Thought 3: As for my "should" belief- yes it would have been good if he was watching but the fact is he wasn't and insisting now that he watch what already has happened doesn't make any sense. This is a classic example of an irrational should.

Thought 4: My belief that someone is always trying to get in my way is an overgeneralization because there are certainly times when no one is trying to get in my way. Sometimes people do get in our way, but not always.

Thought 5: I go on to tell myself that I can't stand this, nor will I tolerate this "crap." The truth is I can stand it though I didn't like it, and I'm not really sure what the words "this crap" refers to. Perhaps I was thinking that it was an inconvenience (which it might have been), but I don't think it was "crap."

Thoughts 6 & 7: Finally I end up by fortune telling by predicting that I will now be late (which I don't know yet) and I catastrophize by thinking it "sucks" and is "terrible". Actually nothing got sucked and this mishap was not the end of the world.

Conclusion
At this point we recognize that our thoughts cause our emotions, and as the above case demonstrated irrational

thinking can lead to feeling of anger, anxiety and potentially violent and threatening behavior. We also can now identify the various types of irrational thinking that were going on in the road rage example.

In this chapter we learned that it is not enough to be able to tell a rational thought from an irrational thought. This chapter presented the many ways that a thought can be irrational. Most importantly we now recognize and swallow the bitter pill that sometimes, some of our thoughts are irrational.

We've come a long way in understanding where our emotions come from and knowing the difference between rational and irrational thinking. But there's one more bitter pill that we have to swallow.

thinking can lead to feeling of anger, anxiety and potentially violent and threatening behavior. We also can now identify the various types of irrational thinking that were going on in the road rage example.

In this chapter we learned that it is not enough to be able to tell a rational thought from an irrational thought. This chapter presented the many ways that a thought can be irrational. Most importantly we now recognize and swallow the bitter pill that sometimes, some of our thoughts are irrational.

We've come a long way in understanding where our emotions come from and knowing the difference between rational and irrational thinking. But there's one more bitter pill that we have to swallow.

Chapter Seven: The Fourth Bitter Pill - Talk back to Your Irrational Thoughts

The bitter pill that you have to swallow now is the act of arguing with your irrational thoughts. You have accepted that you can't change someone else, but you can change the way you feel and behave. You understand that your thoughts cause your feelings and you have even begun to see that according to the criteria for a rational thought some of your thoughts are IRRATIONAL. You have swallowed the first three bitter pills. Now you have to talk back to your irrational thoughts and replace them with rational thoughts.

It is not enough to say "just stop thinking irrational thoughts." There is a principle of science that "nature abhors a vacuum." That means that if you try to remove something that is in place and has been in place for any length of time, you will find that it can't be done. You can't simply tell yourself not to think irrational thoughts. You also can't just tell yourself to not think. Try it and see. Your brain is a thinking machine and you can't just turn it off. So instead you have to make your brain do something different. By replacing irrational thoughts with rational thoughts we make our brains do something different.

This is work and it does take effort. Like many things in life, you will get out of this what you put into it. As I stated early on, this requires effort on your part. You have to take an active role in Cognitive Behavioral SELF Therapy.

Here's how we talk back to our irrational thoughts. Remember my example of road rage in the last chapter? If you'll recall I had presented a situation where another car came very close to mine and I had to slam on the brakes. That was the event that I was aware of (A). I then had several thoughts rapidly fire through my brain (B). They were mostly irrational. Those thoughts then triggered my feelings (C) of anger and anxiety. As a further consequence of those feelings I shook my fist and threw the finger (more C).

Below is a list of the irrational thoughts (on the left) presented in the road rage example presented in the last chapter. Those came from the B column of the ABC's. In the right hand column I have added what we could call **Rational refutations.** Albert Ellis who is considered to be the grandfather of Cognitive Therapy, sometimes added a D to the ABC's. Ellis said that the D stood for *disputing* the irrational thoughts. These disputes are rational alternative thoughts to answer the irrational thoughts. We are simply going to replace our previously held irrational thought with a rational thought or dispute that meets the criteria for a rational thought as presented in Chapter 5.

Irrational Thoughts	Rational Thoughts (Disputes/Refutations)
1) That guy almost killed me (all or none thinking)	1) He came very close to hitting my car but didn't. I'm okay.
2) He's an S.O.B. (irrational labeling)	2) He's a man who might not have seen me. He couldn't be the son of a female dog.
3) He should've been watching where he was going (Irrational Should)	3) It doesn't seem like he saw me. I wonder if he was distracted.
4) Someone's always trying to get in my way (Overgeneralization)	4) Sometimes these things happen. I'm not sure he meant to get in my way.

Four "Bitter Pills" For Feeling Better Fast

5) I can't stand this. I won't tolerate this crap. (Can't-Stand-It-it is)	5) This scared me but I'm okay. I guess this is a risk of the road.
6) Now I'll be late. This will ruin my whole day. (Fortune telling)	6)This was a brief delay but now it's time to get on with the rest of my day.
7) This sucks. It's terrible (Catastrophizing)	This was unfortunate and scary, but everything is okay.

Do the Rational thoughts (Disputes/Refutations) presented in the right hand column above fit the criteria for RATIONAL thoughts?

Criteria for A RATIONAL THOUGHT;
    1.   is supported by objective fact
    2.   helps you maintain your physical health and well being
    3.   helps you reduce conflict with people you care about
    4.   helps you accomplish a task or goal that is important to you
    5.   helps you feel calm, accepting, at peace

It's clear to see that each of the new thoughts (disputes/refutations) meets all of the criteria for rational thinking.

    In this particular case the criteria of reducing conflict with people I care about may not apply. The other driver is a stranger to me and so I might say that I don't really care about him. However, if we consider a crash or a physical altercation to be a form of conflict, then my new rational

Four "Bitter Pills" For Feeling Better Fast

thoughts might help me avoid further conflict. When I correct my irrational label of the other driver being an "SOB" or a "jackass" or any other name we could think of to call him, I stop dehumanizing him and begin to think of him as a person just like me. This is what is meant by "toning down the rhetoric."

As you look at the rational thoughts (which refute my previous irrational thoughts) do you see how the rational thoughts could have the consequence of calming a person down? That is exactly what happens. By changing the way we think about a situation we change the way we feel.

You might think it's not that easy. I agree with you that at first it might not be easy. Any new skill you learn to do usually isn't easy the first few times you do it. However, with some practice and repetition your new found skill becomes easier and more familiar. The key is to not give up before you even give it a try.

Once you develop the ability to refute your previously held irrational beliefs by replacing them with rational beliefs/thoughts you can begin to talk back to those thoughts. This is where the real therapy is taking place and you do it to yourself. That's why it's called Cognitive Behavioral SELF Therapy.

EXERCISE-Disputing irrational thoughts
As a way to practice disputing irrational thoughts what follows is an exercise to give you some practice. I encourage you to not rush through this exercise, as this is a crucial step in helping yourself to feel better. I will present what the **Awareness of the event** was, and then give you the irrational Belief/Thought, Consequences, and Dispute/Refutations columns. Your job will be to fill in

alternative rational thoughts to dispute the irrational thoughts. In the first example I have provided sample disputes/refutations.

Example 1
Awareness of Event- My friend Jack said that I owed him money for knocking down his mailbox when I backed out of his driveway last week.

Irrational Belief/Thought	Consequences	Rational Thoughts (Disputes/Refutations)
1) He's out of his mind (mind reading) 2) He's always accusing me of something (overgeneralization) 3) He's a raving lunatic (irrational labeling) 4) If I have to pay him for his mailbox our friendship is over (confusing choice with having to) 5) I shouldn't have gone out with him to the hockey game (irrational should)	Anger Anxiety Told him I wouldn't give him the money.	1) I can't read his mind so I don't know if he's out of it. 2) There are some times when he doesn't accuse me and he's a good friend. 3) I can understand that he's upset about his mailbox being knocked down. 4) I might choose to help him with his mailbox but I don't have to. 5) We had a good time at the game and I had fun until the mailbox incident.

Example 2
Awareness of Event- My wife did not do a task I had asked her to take care of.

Irrational Belief/Thoughts	Consequences	Rational Thoughts (Disputes/Refutations)
1) She never does what I ask (Overgeneralization) 2) This proves she doesn't love me (Mind reading) 3) I need her to take care of this (Confusing needs and wants) 4) She should've taken care of this (Irrational Should statement)	Anger Depression Yelled and left the house	1) 2) 3) 4)

Example 3
Awareness of Event- My son did not empty the dishwasher as I had asked him to do.

Irrational Belief/Thought	Consequences	Rational Thoughts (Disputes/Refutations)
1) He's a lazy nitwit (Irrational Label) 2) He should listen to his father	Anger Depression Guilt Yelled at him	1) 2)

(Irrational should) 3) He'll never amount to anything (Overgeneralization) 4) I guess I'll have to do it (Confusing having to with choosing to) 5) I guess I'm unable to let him drive the car (Confusing unable with unwilling)	and took the car away for a week	3) 4) 5)

Example 4

Awareness of Event- My boss told me that after six years with my employer I was going to lose my job due to a restructuring of the company

Irrational Belief/Thoughts	Consequences	Rational Thoughts (Disputes/Refutations)
1) My boss is a jackass for laying me off (Irrational Label) 2) My life sucks (All or none thinking) 3) I'll never get another job (Fortune telling) 4)I'll lose my	Anger Anxiety Depression Told my boss she was a liar and had no integrity and then walked out of the meeting	1) 2) 3) 4)

Four "Bitter Pills" For Feeling Better Fast

home now (more fortune telling) 5) This is the worst day of my life (Catastrophizing) 6) Someone else should get laid off (Irrational should)		5) 6)

Example 5

Awareness of Event- My daughter who is a pre-med student received a grade of C in her Organic Chemistry class in college. When we spoke on the phone she told me that it was okay and that it didn't matter.

Irrational Belief/Thoughts	Consequences	Rational Thoughts (Disputes/Refutations)
1) She has no idea what she's talking about (Mind reading) 2) She'll never get into medical school now (Fortune telling) 3) I didn't raise her with the right values (Overgeneralization) 4) This is awful (Catastrophizing)	Anger Anxiety Guilt Ended the conversation and hung up	1) 2) 3) 4)

Hopefully, you are able to dispute the irrational thoughts that have been presented above. Talk back to the thoughts by coming up with a rational alternative. Remember that your rational dispute should meet the criteria for a rational thought which was presented earlier in this chapter. If you can dispute the irrational thoughts of someone else in the examples above, then soon you should be able to talk back to your own irrational thinking.

If you've made it this far in this book that's great. At this point I would suggest you go back to the QUICK START GUIDE TO FEELING BETTER and review each of the steps. It is important that you understand how this works as you begin to develop rational thinking skills. If there is something that doesn't make sense to you go back and reread that section.

Case Example
Let's take a look at a case example of a recent client who came to see me and how Cognitive Behavioral SELF Therapy worked for her.

Susan was an intelligent 35 year old married woman who had three children under the age of 8. She came to therapy because she wanted help learning to cope with her boss. One of the first things she told me was that she didn't want me to tell her to leave her job, because all her friends were telling her to quit. Instead, she was hoping that I could help her learn how to make her boss behave better. (She wanted me to engage in the conspiracy to change someone else's behavior).

At the first appointment Susan had many of the symptoms of a moderate to severe level of depression. She frequently cried during the session, and admitted to crying often. She had trouble sleeping, had lost her appetite, had little sexual desire, and said she felt depressed and anxious. She also said she wasn't enjoying her time with her family. She said she liked the freedom her job gave her, but that she found her boss difficult to work for because he often ridiculed his employees publically, and was highly critical of the way they got their jobs done. According to her, the boss was quite demanding.

Within the first three counseling sessions Susan began doing some ABC's and began to accept that her feelings were being caused not by her boss, but by the thoughts she had about her boss. Below is an example of what one of her ABC homework assignments looked like.

A	B	C
Awareness/Event	**Belief/Thought about the Event**	**Consequences (Emotions/Behaviors)**
Boss yelling Critical of work done	1) He treats us like this because he's from another country 2) I can't stand being spoken to like this 3) He shouldn't talk to his employees like this 4) Some of my coworkers	Depression Anxiety Anger Guilt Crying on the way home from work Passivity

	can't handle him the way I can 5) I need to take this abuse because I need this job and I don't want to have to get another job 6) I have to try to see this from his point of view	

Once we identified some of the thoughts she was having, Susan began to apply the five criteria for rational thinking to her own thoughts. She quickly realized that not one of these thoughts was rational. All of these thoughts were either not in keeping with objective fact, not helping her to meet her goal of doing her job to her satisfaction, not helping her to feel the way she wanted to, and not helping her to avoid conflict with someone she cared about (her boss). Her irrational thinking was also having an indirect effect on her physical health as she was having sleep problems and had lost some weight due to a decreased appetite and her sexual desire was diminished, all due to her depression.

Susan agreed these thoughts were irrational and that she was making herself miserable. She realized that the fact that her boss was from a different country was no excuse for him to talk to his employees the way he did. This thought was an **overgeneralization**. She acknowledged that she knew other people from other countries who didn't talk to people the way her boss did.

She also recognized that telling herself that she "couldn't stand" being spoken too like this wasn't true (**Can't stand it-itis**). She could stand it and in fact had been standing it for some time now.

She also realized that saying or thinking to herself that "he shouldn't talk to his employees like this" flew in the face that he WAS talking to his employees the way he was. This was an **irrational should** statement. That thought wasn't helpful.

She came to realize that how her coworkers handled him really didn't have anything to do with how she preferred to be treated. This was some **mind reading** of her coworkers.

Susan recognized her thought that she needed this job was a case of her **confusing needs and wants**. She wanted the job for it's flexibility but she didn't need the job.

Finally, she came to realize that she didn't need to see it from his point of view (**confusing choosing to with having to**). This was about her point of view, and her thoughts about how she was being treated. She didn't have to see it from his point of view.

Susan quickly learned to evaluate her thinking using the 5 criteria for a rational thought. Once she acknowledged her irrational thoughts she was able to identify them according to what types they were. Once she did this I asked her what she was going to do. She responded that she would go to work and the next time he spoke to her like this, she would tell him "You can't talk to people like this." I suggested to her that was just like saying 'he shouldn't talk to his employees like this." I explained to Susan that her boss could speak to his employees any way he wanted to. He could even be more offensive if he wanted to.

Susan sank back into her chair as if she had been defeated. But it seemed like she really began to think more rationally about the situation as she remained quite in her thoughts for a couple of minutes. Then she said "I'm going to tell him that I won't be spoken to like that again." She went on to say she didn't want to be spoken to like that anymore. Finally she was having a rational thought. But not only was it a rational thought, it was a thought that she could put into action.

The next time I saw Susan she told me that during the past week her boss had harshly reprimanded her for the way she completed a function on the computer. He had grabbed the mouse out of her hand and did it the way he thought it should be done. Susan proudly told me about how she remained calm when he did this and thought to herself that she didn't want to be spoken to this way. In a quite but firm voice she told him "I won't put up with you talking to me like this." She even went on to tell him that she would walk out of the office immediately if he didn't stop.

Her boss stopped and put the mouse down and then walked away to do something else. Susan believes that her response to her boss had a big impact on the quality of their interactions during the next week. Susan also said she felt much better and more confident about going to work.

The most important thing to happen here was that Susan saw the connection between her irrational and rational thoughts, and how she felt and behaved. By changing her irrational misery producing thoughts into rational calming thoughts, she was able to express to her boss that she was not going to put up with being spoken to this way. She changed her feeling to being empowered and calm, and her behavior followed accordingly. Her rational thinking helped transform her behavior and her relationship with her boss. Eventually, Susan decided to look for another job and gave her boss her four weeks notice when she found a position she thought would be more to her liking.

As is often the case when we have a tendency towards irrational thoughts in one situation, we tend to have them in many. Susan also had similar thoughts about her relationship with her husband. With continued practice she began to identify her irrational thoughts in other situations and then worked to replace them with rational thoughts. Susan got very good at recognizing her own irrational thinking and correcting it. In a very short period of time she began to feel more calm and less depressed and anxious. She stopped having crying spells and began to communicate more effectively with her boss, her husband, her family and friends. Her mood improved, and her appetite and sleep returned to normal.

Susan commented that she was surprised how quickly she was relieved of her miserable feelings. She had thought that she would need to be in therapy for a long time, and that it would be a painful process. She thought that she would need to bring up painful memories about her childhood, and that those memories were somehow causing some of her current depression. Instead her new way of thinking helped her put her childhood experiences into rational perspective. She began applying these new skills in all areas of her life and became a believer in the practice of Cognitive Behavioral SELF Therapy.

Conclusion

In this chapter we discussed the bitter pill of talking back to our irrational thoughts. Talking back to your irrational thoughts is how you help yourself feel calm, and behave in a calm and self controlled manner. By being able to recognize just how your thinking can sometimes be irrational, you can substitute a rational thought for your formerly held irrational belief. This is an active process and you have to be willing to do it to yourself. Remember, you can't make someone else change, and someone else can't make you change.

By recognizing that your thoughts cause your emotions and engaging in the active process of refuting your irrational thoughts (which cause your unwanted emotions) you can help yourself feel much better and have more effective interactions with the people in your life.

Chapter Eight: A Prediction and A Challenge

I hope I'm wrong about this. Maybe I'm mind reading. In therapy what sometimes happens is my clients learn the basics of Cognitive Behavioral SELF Therapy and once they have humored me by listening to how it works and how it can make them feel better, it *seems* that they then set it aside. It *seems* like after they have heard about it, it's time to move on and get back to talking about how someone or something else is making them miserable. Or they want to learn how they can change someone else.

Now that you've read this far I predict that you might do the same thing (This is fortune telling- an irrational thought because I don't know what you'll do). You'll put the book up on your shelf but more sadly you'll put the ideas away too. This might become just another technique you read about at some time in the past like when you wanted to learn about food preservation or how to fix something in your home. I hope I'm wrong about this but I do see it happen often (Just because I might see it happen with others doesn't mean it will happen with you- that's anecdotal evidence, another irrational thought).

Some of my clients will argue that they are so accustomed to thinking irrationally that they are incapable of thinking rationally. Of course this is an irrational thought too because it is an overgeneralization. It's like they are saying that they always think irrationally and they never think rationally. A more rational way to think about this is that sometimes you think rationally and sometimes you think irrationally. Therefore you *can* do this. Be careful to not confuse your perceived *inability* with an *unwillingness* to talk back to your irrational thoughts.

Four "Bitter Pills" For Feeling Better Fast

You might think that this change will be difficult for you, or you might think that the Cognitive Behavioral SELF Therapy approach is *too* simple and won't help you with your complex problem. If we go back to our ABC's it might look like this:

A	B	C
Awareness/Event	**Belief/Thought about the Event**	**Consequences (Emotions/Behaviors)**
Heard therapist explain Cognitive Behavioral SELF Therapy/ Read Book	"This sounds fairly straight forward but I think it will be hard to do" "This seems too simple. My problems are more complex" "This won't work for my problems"	Anxiety (Uncertainty) Depression (Doubt) Don't follow through on doing home work exercises Drop out of therapy

This is how many people prematurely give up on implementing Cognitive therapy before seeing the benefits of this approach. They have talked themselves right out of trying to do something different. Perhaps they still haven't swallowed the first bitter pill and they are still hoping that therapy can help them learn how to change someone else.

Sometimes these clients tell themselves that therapy isn't for them. They might go see a different therapist sometime in the future when their distress intensifies again. Other clients talk themselves out of therapy by thinking it's *too* hard. I frequently tell my clients that changing the way they think does not necessarily have to be difficult.

I once had a client who came to see me after being out of therapy with another therapist many years ago. This woman had begun feeling depressed and anxious recently and many years before her depression and anxiety had been so severe that she required hospitalization. Eventually, she underwent some outpatient counseling and began to feel much better for several years, until the past few months before she contacted me. As I began to discuss cognitive therapy with her, I saw her facial expression brighten and it seemed like her eyes lit up. She had worked with a therapist before who was cognitively oriented and she felt the approach had been very helpful. She admitted that she had discontinued using what she had previously learned in therapy. She had gone back to thinking that other people, places and things caused her misery, and over time she had gotten herself into thinking she was helpless to change the way she felt and acted. But very quickly she brushed up her Cognitive Behavioral SELF Therapy skills, and within three sessions her mood greatly improved, and she needed my services no more.

As I said before Cognitive Behavioral SELF Therapy is like the game of chess or Othello. It can be learned very quickly, but it takes a lifetime to master. That is not meant to discourage you but instead is intended to encourage you to keep working on rational thinking. We are all "works in progress" and by continuing to employ the basic principles

Four "Bitter Pills" For Feeling Better Fast

presented in this book I firmly believe you will become more calm and content in your life and not be as upset by the things that happen in your life.

Please give yourself the chance to put into practice what you have read about. I would challenge you to make an intentional effort to employ the ideas presented here for the next four to six months. If after that time you're not seeing the benefit then fine, go back to your previous way or look for a different therapy approach. If you swallow the bitter pills discussed here I think you will feel better and be able to maintain control over your emotions and behaviors.

The secret to continuing to feel better is simple. It's like when your doctor prescribes medication to you. It will help you as long as you keep taking it. Likewise, with Cognitive Behavioral SELF Therapy you have to continue swallowing the four bitter pills.

1. **The First Bitter Pill- You can't change others but you can change you**
2. **The Second bitter pill- Your Thoughts Cause Your Feelings**
3. **The Third bitter pill- Sometimes your thoughts are irrational**
4. **The Fourth Bitter Pill- Talk Back to your Irrational Thoughts**

Appendix A

Here is another ABC form for you to make copies of and use to record your Event, Thoughts, and Emotional and Behavioral Consequences.

A Awareness of the Event	**B** Belief/Thought about the Event	**C** Consequences (Emotional/Behavioral)

Appendix B

In chapter 6 you learned about the ten most common types of irrational thoughts. This list contains all ten of the irrational thought types you have already learned about, and it has 16 additional types of irrational thoughts. I recommend you start with the smaller list of irrational thought types to monitor in yourself, and once you master those you can add some of these.

1) All or None Thinking- black or white thinking. Thinking something is all good or all bad.
2) Overgeneralization- thoughts that use words like "always" or "never" These thoughts fail to consider sometimes, occasionally, often and rarely?
3) Mental Filter*- acknowledging only what matches with what you believe.
4) Discounting the Positive- failure to recognize something positive aspects of the situation
5) Jumping to Conclusions- forming an opinion without having any facts. Two forms of this include:
    Mind Reading- attributing thoughts and intentions to another person
    Fortune Telling- predicting the future like you know what will happen
6) Magnification/Minimization- exaggerating a shortcoming or minimizing a good quality
7) Emotional Reasoning- belief that because you feel something strongly it must be so
8) Irrational Labeling- inaccurate labeling "He's a jackass"
9) Personalization and Blame- inaccurately assuming the cause for something

Four "Bitter Pills" For Feeling Better Fast

10) Irrational Should Statements- usually with regards to events in the past, demands, musts, oughts and "rules" which aren't followed by others

11) Confusing Needs with Wants- our absolute needs are water, food, shelter and sleep. Everything else is a want.

12) Confusing Choosing To (Choice) with Having To (Force)- we are rarely physically forced to do anything. We usually choose to do things even when we say "we have to"

13) Can't Stand-it-itis- if we say we can't stand it does that mean we'll explode? As bad as it is we could probably stand some more

14) Catastrophizing- "awful, terrible, horrible." Ultimately we all have one day in life that is completely awful, terrible and horrible. It's usually the same day that we can't stand it anymore.

15) Magical Worry- The irrational belief that by worrying about something it might not happen or that we can prevent the thing we are worrying about from happening.

16) Having Irrational Definitions- "I'm a failure because I failed the test."

17) Confusing Relying on with Depending on- relying on someone to do something you can do vs. depending on someone to do something you can't do.

18) Confusing Inability with Unwillingness- confusion about our ability vs. our desire to do something

19) Confusing Possibility with Probability- a pseudo scientific form of fortune telling. Just because something is possible does not mean it is probable.

20) Projection- because you believe something, you attribute it to others. "Because I'm not always honest I'll bet he's lying to me."

21) Being Upset About an "Idea" Rather than the "Facts"- belief that a situation requires/demands us to be upset regardless of the consequences of the situation. We're supposed to be upset.

22) Nonsense Arguments- the "historical if"- "If only it hadn't happened"... But it did

23) Irrational Hopelessness/Helplessness- Convincing yourself to give up because there can't possibly be a solution or another way.

24) Too Much/Too Little Problem- believing the concept of too much/too little actually exists in reality. Is it possible to have too much money? Where is the exact line between too much or too little and just enough?

25) Ambivalent Beliefs- contradictory beliefs that prevent us from doing anything about it the situation

26) Correlation Equals Causation- because two things happen at the same time does not mean one causes the other. Anecdotal evidence makes for lousy scientific method.

upset regardless of the consequences of the situation. We're supposed to be upset.

22) Nonsense Arguments- the "historical if"- "If only it hadn't happened". . . But it did

23) Irrational Hopelessness/Helplessness- Convincing yourself to give up because there can't possibly be a solution or another way.

24) Too Much/Too Little Problem- believing the concept of too much/too little actually exists in reality. Is it possible to have too much money? Where is the exact line between too much or too little and just enough?

25) Ambivalent Beliefs- contradictory beliefs that prevent us from doing anything about it the situation

26) Correlation Equals Causation- because two things happen at the same time does not mean one causes the other. Anecdotal evidence makes for lousy scientific method.

References

Beck, A.T. (1979). *Cognitive Therapy of Depression.* New York, NY, Guilford Press

Burns, David D. (1980). *Feeling Good The New Mood Therapy.* New York, NY, Avon Books.

Ellis, Albert, (1999) *How to Make Yourself Happy and Remarkably Less Disturbable,* Impact Publishers

Ellis, Albert, (1962) *Reason and Emotion in Psychotherapy*

Maultsby, Maxie (1990). *Rational Behavior Therapy,* Appleton, WI, Rational Self-Help Aids/I'ACT

Pucci, Aldo, R. (2006) *The Client's Guide to Cognitive-Behavioral Therapy,* Lincoln, NE, iUniverse

About the Author

For over 23 years Mr. Michener has provided therapy services in a variety of settings. He attended St. John Fisher College in Rochester, NY where he was initially introduced to Cognitive Behavior Therapy, and then went to Syracuse University where he earned an MSW and was trained as a marriage and family therapist. During the 1990's, as a professor of social work he began to reevaluate the benefits of different therapy approaches which led him back to cognitive therapy. He is currently in private practice and operates an Employee Assistance Program in Rochester, NY. Mr. Michener has been married for over 23 years, and is a father to three children.

Breinigsville, PA USA
01 December 2010
250429BV00004B/197/P

9 781601 457202